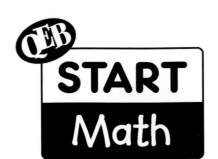

START
Math

Counting
Book 2

Ann Montague-Smith

QEB Publishing

Published in the United States by

QEB Publishing, Inc.
23062 La Cadena Drive
Laguna Hills
Irvine
CA 92653

Library of Congress Control Number: 2004102070

ISBN 1-59566-028-3

Written by Ann Montague-Smith
Designed and edited by The Complete Works
Illustrated by Jenny Tulip
Photography by Steve Lumb and Michael Wicks

Creative Director Louise Morley
Editorial Manager Jean Coppendale

Printed and bound in China

With thanks to:

Contents

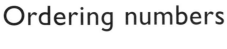

Matching numbers 1 to 5

Match the numbers to the sets of candy.

1

2

3

4

5

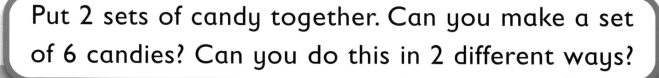

Put 2 sets of candy together. Can you make a set of 6 candies? Can you do this in 2 different ways?

Challenge

Find some toys.
Count out a set of 1.
Now do this again for 2.
Make all the sets from 1 to 5.

Matching numbers 1 to 8

Match the numbers to the animals.

Put 2 sets of animals together. Can you make a set of 8? Can you find 2 different ways to do this?

6

4

8

3

Challenge

Look through this book. Can you
find the number 1? Now find a number
2. Find all the numbers through 8.

Matching numbers 1 to 10

Match the numbers to the bugs.

(1) (2) (3) (4) (5) (6) (7) (8) (9) (10)

Put sets together and count them all.
Find 2 different ways to make 10.

Challenge

Draw your own sets
of bugs.
Draw 8 bugs.
Now draw 9 bugs.
Can you draw 10 bugs?

9

Introducing zero

Which numbers can you find?

Get some paper and a crayon.
Write all the numbers you can find.

10

Challenge

Draw some cars. Count how many. Write the number. Do this again for different numbers of cars.

Estimating

Get some blocks and some board game tokens. Take a handful of blocks and put them on your field. Ask your friend to guess how many there are. If your friend guesses the right number, she puts a token on her number strip. Now switch roles.

1 2 3 4 5

The winner is the first one to collect 5 tokens.

Challenge

Play the game again. This time use a number strip with 1 to 10 on it.

| 1 | 2 | 3 | 4 | 5 |

Finding 1 more and 1 fewer

Count the pairs of sets of balloons.
Which set has 1 more?
Which set has 1 fewer?

Which set of balloons has 1 more than 6?
Which set of balloons has 1 fewer than 9?

Challenge

Put out 8 toys.
Now make another set of toys with 1 fewer than 8.
How many toys would there be if there were 1 more than 8?

15

More and fewer

Are there enough homes for the pets?

Are there more dogs or more doghouses?

Are there fewer rabbits or fewer hutches?

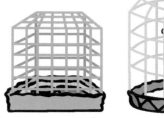

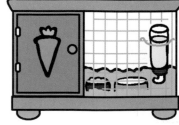

Which set has the most animals?

Which set has the fewest animals?

Challenge

Make sets with
1 to 10 toys in them.
Which set has
the most toys?
Which set has
the fewest toys?

The mailman can't deliver the mail.

The houses are in the wrong order.

Can you tell the mailman which house is first?

Now which comes second? And the next one?

6 **1** **3** **4** **8** **2** **9**

18

Which house should come last?

Challenge

Play this with a friend. Get a set of cards with 1 to 10 on them. Take turns to turn over a card. Decide where the card should go. Make a line of cards which read from 1 to 10.

Missing numbers

The kids' t-shirts are mixed up.
Match the number of fingers they are showing to the right t-shirt. One t-shirt is missing its number.
What number should it be?

Can you write the missing number on some paper?

Challenge
Draw 1 toy.
Write the number.
Do the same for all the
numbers through 10.
Make sure you write the
numbers in order.

3

6

4

8

Supporting notes for adults

Matching numbers 1 to 5 – pages 4-5

Read the numbers together. Now ask the children to count each set and match it to its number. Encourage them to point and count. If children find this difficult, they can touch and count.

Matching numbers 1 to 8 – pages 6-7

Have the children read the numbers, then count each set of animals. Encourage them to point to the relevant number as they count the sets.

Matching numbers 1 to 10 – pages 8-9

Encourage the children to read the numbers in order, so that they are counting up to 10. Encourage them to count each set. Since the bugs are small, they might need to touch and count to do this. Tell them to remember which bugs have been counted so far, and which have not been counted yet.

Introducing zero – pages 10-11

There is a zero, 0, in this activity. Encourage the children to find it. If they are not sure what a zero looks like, draw one for them. Ask them to make a zero in the air, with a whole arm movement. This will help to reinforce their memory of its shape.

Estimating – pages 12-13

Explain that estimating, or guessing, means that you do not count. Ask the children to look quickly at how many blocks they have and make their guess. Then they can check by counting. The Challenge activity can extend the game into using larger numbers.

Finding 1 more and 1 fewer – pages 14-15

Encourage the children to count the sets of balloons in pairs. Now ask, "Which set has 1 more? Which set has 1 fewer?"

More and fewer – pages 16-17

Ask the children to count each pair: the animals and their homes. Ask, "Are there more… ? Which set has fewer?" Encourage the children to count by pointing. Those who find this difficult can touch and count.

Ordering numbers – pages 18-19

If the children are not sure of ordinal numbers, help them by asking, "Which is first/second/third… ?"

Missing numbers – pages 20-21

Ask the children to count how many fingers each child has up. Now ask them to match 1 finger to the t-shirt with 1 on it, and so on. The missing number is 10.

Suggestions for using this book

Children will enjoy looking through the book and talking about the colorful pictures. Sit somewhere comfortable together. Read the instructions to them, then encourage them to take part in the activity and check whether or not they understand what to do.

When children see the written numbers, have them read each one out loud. They will find it helpful to find other examples of written 1, 2, 3… around them, such as finding the page numbers in this book, finding these numbers in another book, on the clock, etc. This will help you to be sure that they recognize and can read the numbers. Encourage them to write how many things there are. At first they may make dots, draw boxes, etc. to show how many there are. Encourage them to form the numbers by using large arm movements in the air and writing with crayons or paint.

There are activities where children are encouraged to estimate "how many." Encourage the children to guess, and remember, no guess is "wrong"! The goal is for children to become more accurate in their estimates through practical experience of estimating, then counting to check. When they can make reasonable estimates for up to 10 objects, try providing smaller things to pick up, such as board game tokens or buttons, so that they can extend their skills for estimating and counting beyond 10.

The vocabulary of counting is extended to include "more" and "fewer," and ordinal numbers. Ask, "How many more are there here… than here?" Then ask the children to count up from the smaller set to the larger one, keeping track on their fingers. This will tell them how many more there are. Similarly, for "fewer," they can either count up from the smaller set, or count back from the larger one.